What if Night?

KEYSTONE
CANYON PRESS

Keystone Canyon Press
2341 Crestone Drive
Reno, NV 89523

www.keystonecanyon.com

A Cataloging-in-Publication record for this title is available from the Library of Congress.

ISBN 978-1-953055-01-9
EPUB ISBN 978-1-953055-03-3

Manufactured in South Korea

What if Night?

by Paul Bogard • illustrated by Sarah Holden

KEYSTONE
CANYON PRESS

What if night never came?
Wouldn't that be great?

You wouldn't have to go to bed. Ever!

You could stay outside and play, forever.

Wouldn't life without night be amazing?

4

Maybe.
For a little while.

But where would the moon go to shine its light?

Where would the stars appear
if the sky were always bright?

What about the birds
who travel far in the dark?

Or the crickets with their music,
or the fireflies with their spark?

All around the world, in forests
and deserts and oceans and plains . . .

For creatures tiny to creatures huge . . .

When the day grows dark,
life really begins.

13

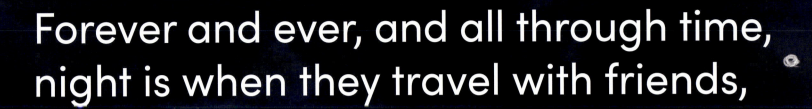

Forever and ever, and all through time,
night is when they travel with friends,

or find their favorite food,
or stop to sing to stars.

So, what would all the animals who need darkness do, if night never came?

16

What about you,
when you grow tired,
how would you sleep?

17

When would you dream …

Of all the places you want to visit, all the fun things you will do?

Now, here is some good news:

As long as the world keeps spinning, night will always arrive.

And you can help,
by turning off the light …

In your garden, at your back door,
or even in your room.

All the life that finds a home in darkness
will have a chance to thrive,

24

And so will you.

Questions for Young Readers

- Can you imagine what your life would be like without night?
- Which animals did you recognize in the book? (Hint: Don't forget about the birds and insects.)
- Why do you think so many animals are active at night? Why is darkness important to them?
- Why do people need nighttime and darkness?
- Can you see the stars in the night sky where you live? Can you count them?
- What can you and your family do to protect the darkness at night? (Hint: think about the lights outside your home.)
- Where else do you see bright lights at night?
- What can you share with your friends about the importance of darkness at night?

Do You Know?

- Doctors have learned that light at night makes people sleep less and have less energy during the day.
- Many birds migrate at night. Bright lights can draw them off course and cause them to get lost.
- Baby sea turtles are confused by bright streetlights and buildings and crawl toward those lights, instead of out to sea as they should.
- Many insects are nocturnal (active at night) and many more are crepuscular (most active at dawn and dusk). Light pollution disrupts their usual patterns of eating, flying, and hiding.

To Learn More . . .

Artificial light has revolutionized the way we live and work at night, but it has come at a price. When used indiscriminately, outdoor lighting can disrupt wildlife, impact human health, waste money and energy, contribute to climate change, and block our view of the universe.

- The International Dark-Sky Association works to raise awareness of the many costs of light pollution and to offer thoughtful solutions. Please visit their website to find out more: www.darksky.org.
- Many other organizations are dedicated to working on behalf of creatures that depend on the night, including Bat Conservation International and The National Audubon Society (for birds). They will always welcome hearing from you.
- If you want to see a night sky full of stars, consider a visit to a national park. For information about parks in the USA, visit www.nps.gov and search for "Protecting the Night."